Grandma Knows Best, But No One Ever Listens!

Mary McBride

Illustrations by Christine Tripp

Meadowbrook
Distributed by Simon and Schuster
New York

Dedication

To my mother, who, in her role as grandmother, gave my children beautiful memories they will carry with them always

Acknowledgment

Deep appreciation is expressed to my daughter, Veronica McBride, whose many contributions to this book have been invaluable.

Library of Congress Cataloging-in-Publication Data

McBride, Mary
    Grandma knows best — but no one ever listens.

    1. Grandmothers — Anecdotes, facetiae, satire, etc.
2. Grandparent and child — Anecdotes, facetiae, satire, etc.
I. Title.

PN6231.G8M33   1987   818'.5402   87-1575
ISBN 0-88166-094-9 (priced)
ISBN 0-88166-097-3 (unpriced)
ISBN 0-671-63622-7 (Simon & Schuster)

Published by Meadowbrook Press, 5451 Smetana Drive, Minnetonka, MN 55343. Book Trade Distribution by Simon and Schuster, a division of Simon & Schuster, Inc., 1230 Avenue of the Americas, New York, NY 10020.

S&S Ordering: 0-671-63622-7 (priced)

02 01 00 99   26 25 24 23

Printed in the United States of America.

Author: Mary McBride
Editor: Bruce Lansky
Illustrations: Christine Tripp
Art Director: Mary Foster
Design: Jill Rogers
Cover Design: Terry Dugan
Keyline: Scott Stoddard
Production: Nanci Jean Stoddard

Contents

Foreword

On the way to the delivery room, I almost changed my mind about having a baby.

I wouldn't have found it so hard to go ahead with if I had realized that having a baby was the only way I could ever become a grandmother.

Becoming a grandmother is the ultimate happiness. Just when you've settled for being an ordinary person, you find out you're a super person, because a grandchild comes along who holds that opinion.

Of course, it isn't all storybook stuff. Grandchildren are young, and they need training. Unfortunately, grandmother has to sit on the sidelines and let people who are not nearly as capable do the job.

We used to spank them when they threw tantrums. Nowadays, they've all had color analysis, and the mother will say, "Blue is not your color, honey, so don't hold your breath."

Expect a little misery. A grandchild is apt to see your varicose veins as an ideal race course for toy cars. She may pull your turtleneck into a cowl. No doubt, you'll find your grandchild's favorite thumb-sucking blanket two hours after the family has driven off. And you're sure to be dismayed by the mud castles they build around your plants. It's all part of the wonderful experience of being a grandmother.

True, grandmothering is not a full-time occupation. A grandmother can send a child home when she feels a gray hair coming on. But it's not a role for the faint-hearted.

It is about time that something was written to help grandmothers. In this book, Mary McBride tells how to scheme, lie, cheat, and threaten so you'll be thought of as a sweet, gentle, darling grandma.

Phyllis Diller

Introduction

So You're Going to Be a Grandmother?

From the day of the announcement,
There is nothing on earth
That seems as important
As the upcoming birth.

You always remember exactly what you were doing when you got the news that you were going to be a grandmother. It's the most wonderful phone call you will ever receive. It may be the only call during which you ignore your "call-waiting" signal.

It doesn't matter how they tell you—whether it's a clever "Are you sitting? Well, you soon will be—on Saturday nights for your grandchild" or just a plain "We're going to have a baby"—the announcement is always a surprise.

One grandmother remarked, "Why, I'm still sending for facts-of-life booklets to find just the right one to give to my daughter."

News that a grandchild is on the way flusters even the most sedate women. If you want to test this, just ask a group of otherwise competent and mature women, "What did you do right after you found out you were going to be a grandmother?"

> "I told everyone I could think of and then decided to have my dripping faucet fixed so I could tell the plumber."

Even the most sedate women come unglued when they get the news.

"I wrote 75 letters saying, 'I want you to be the first to know . . .' "

"I cleared the refrigerator door to make space for drawings."

"I tied tin cans to my car and taped an 'I'M GOING TO BE A GRANDMOTHER' sign to the bumper."

"I practiced diapering the dog and cutting up his dog yummies."

"I blew the dust off my Dr. Spock."

"I painted a 'WELCOME HOME, MOM AND BABY' sign."

"I got so excited, I told my goldfish he was going to become a grandfish."

Occasionally, you may find someone whose anticipation is on the pessimistic side. Upon hearing the good news one grandmother-to-be hung up and put everything breakable up high.

If you suspect news of this sort will be forthcoming, be prepared: Don't drop the phone, or they'll picture you dropping the baby. And be sure not to ask if you were the first grandmother notified.

I
Putting the "Grand" into Grandmothering

Chapter 1

The Grandma Boom

Does becoming a grandma
Leave you aghast?
I'm sorry to say,
Life goes by that fast.

The Baby Boom has spawned an even bigger Grandma Boom. For every baby born, two women turn into grandmas. As a new grandma, you will look in the mirror and think, "I'm too young to be a grandma." But you have to face reality. You are old enough to be a grandma if . . .

Someone calls you "spry."

Someone says, "I hope I'm like you when I'm your age."

When you raise your arm to wave, the flab underneath waves first.

You decide to find a job and discover the references on your last resume are all deceased.

The gate attendant at the airport asks if you want to board first.

The flight attendant says "Watch your step!" to everyone else but takes your arm.

The aerobics instructor looks at you when she says, "Everybody take a rest."

People always pop out of the comfortable chair and offer it to you.

Friends don't call before they stop by, because they expect you to be home.

The things you want to talk about when you see your doctor take more than one sheet of paper.

You don't care what the dentist says about your teeth, as long as he says you can keep them.

Uncle Sam is starting to look young to you.

You always have to ask someone how a television show ended.

Every woman gets a gleam in her eye that wasn't there before she became a grandmother. You never hear anyone say, "If I had to do it over, I would have waited to have grandchildren" or, "I chose not to have grandchildren."

Face reality: you're not too young to be a grandma.

However, don't believe there won't be problems. As a grandmother, you will be one woman alone against her children and their in-laws.

Where do you get assistance in becoming the best grandmother you can be? You can't write for a free booklet from the government or join a grandmother support group. The one thing you can do is pay attention to anyone who gives advice on the subject. Said one grandmother, "There is one general rule any grandmother-to-be would do well to consider . . . . Have another life beyond being a grandmother, but don't let your grandchild know that you do."

Chapter 2

You're Not Getting Older, You're Getting Grandchildren

What a grandma believes
Is quite plain to see:
Her grandchild's the best,
And you'd better agree.

It's not how old you are, it's what you do that makes you a grandmother. You see, grandmothers do certain things that set them apart from other people.

A grandmother . . .

Gets cold in the middle of the night and wonders if her grandchildren are covered.

Feels her grandchild's opinion should be respected—even before he can talk.

Laughs at her grandchild's jokes, even when he gets the punch line wrong.

Starts knitting a layette when a daughter or daughter-in-law says, "We'd like to have one more."

Hears a person say, "What a cute baby!" and replies, "She'll be Miss America someday."

9

Grandmothers say certain things that set them apart from other people.

Laughs heartily at her grandchild's remarks about Grandma being old.

Lets a grandchild take a nap on a $500 bedspread.

Fills the entire raffle book with her grandchildren's names.

Kids love their grandmothers for a variety of reasons. Here are the results of a recent playground poll:
"My grandma . . .

Always buys what I'm selling."

Never puts me on hold when she hears a call-waiting signal."

Never gets tired of asking me words on the spelling list."

Gives me money and never says it has to be saved."

Leaves my drawings up all the time and doesn't just put them up when I'm visiting."

Agrees that my doll *does* need a car seat."

Your grandchildren's parents have a more realistic point of view: "A grandmother is someone who baby-sits."

Chapter 3

Life Is Not a Rerun

How we raised our kids
Made a lot of sense.
But now our best advice
Merely gives offense.

As a grandmother, you need to realize that raising children today is not the same as it was 30 years ago, when you raised children. The tactics you employ when handling grandchildren must be "new and improved."

Lots of changes have cropped up since you were a young mother with all the snappy answers and improved methods:

Parents used to assist with math by showing the child flashcards. Now they help by changing a blown fuse, so the child can continue using the computer.

Children who misbehaved were spanked. Now they are taken to a pediatrician, who refers them to a counselor.

Before, children were raised on Dr. Spock. Now there is a separate book for each problem.

Diapers used to be scrubbed, soaked, and washed. Now they are tossed.

Kids took turns washing and drying dishes. Now they take turns pressing the button on the dishwasher.

On Easter, kids would get chocolate bunnies in green cellophane grass. Now they get molded yogurt bunnies laid in sprouts.

Mothers used to put a little bit of lemon in the shampoo water to lighten their daughters' hair. Now kids' hair is dyed a rainbow of colors.

Kids used to get watches for their high school graduation. Now children wear watches when they enter kindergarten.

Parents had to check with their sons before making vacation plans, so they would not interfere with Little League. Now they have to check both their sons' *and* daughters' sports schedules.

The kids used to fight over who got to lick the beaters. Now frosting comes in a can.

Before, parents would make kids turn off the TV and do their homework. Now kids tape their favorite programs on a VCR.

Thirty years ago children who misbehaved were spanked.

Children had to be on time for meals, or else they got cold food. Now they reheat the food in a microwave.

Teen-agers used to roll their eyes heavenward to show their impatience with parents. Now they can't do that, because they're wearing contact lenses.

Parents used to take children to playgrounds to play on swings and slides. Now most homes are outfitted with swings and slides in their backyards.

Children were constantly being warned, "Look both ways before you cross the street." Now they are driven everywhere and let out at the door.

Despite all the changes, many things remain the same. Babies still get colic and suck their thumbs. Children still miss school buses and mothers drive them to school. Teen-agers still say, "So and so's mother lets her do such and such," and they still talk on the phone for hours. (It's true, there is call-waiting now, but what teen-ager ever hangs up when he or she hears it?)

II
He's Not Naughty, He's My Grandson

Chapter 4

Love Me, Love My Grandchild

If someone would tell me,
"Your grandchild has faults,"
I believe I would call
For my smelling salts.

One grandmother was overheard bragging to the bailiff about her grandson while she was paying his bail. This sort of thing is to be expected, because every grandmother knows her grandchild is wonderful and perfect.

But even the most unrealistic grandmother may, on occasion, have to admit that her darling grandchild is slightly less than perfect. Here are a few dead giveaways:

The dogs at other people's houses beg to go to the basement when you are visiting with him.

His school makes him list at least 10 adults who can be called to come and get him if his parents aren't home.

Your senior citizen center installs a "cry room" just for her.

His art isn't hung on the refrigerator door; it's drawn *right on* the refrigerator door.

The only birthday party he was ever invited to was his own.

Neighboring campers leave their campsites—even when the weather is perfect.

You remove him from church and the congregation applauds.

But a grandmother often refuses to accept reality. Excuses immediately pop into her mind, "explaining" the grandchild's transgressions. Grandmothers have a knack for presenting a grandchild's case so eloquently that even the most doubtful skeptic is convinced of the accused's innocence:

If your grandchild gets anything less than an "A"— "The teacher must give low grades."

If she picks the neighbor's flowers—"They looked just like weeds."

If he plays with his food—"He probably doesn't have enough toys."

Every grandmother knows her grandchild is perfect.

Excuses immediately pop into a grandmother's mind.

If she always gets her shoes on the wrong feet—"She loves to clown around."

If she runs away from home—"The best thing a child can do is become self-reliant."

If he eats his mother's bridge club dessert—"He wants to be part of her social life."

If she is caught copying from someone's paper—"Her posture is so straight her teacher thought she was looking over someone's shoulder."

If he gets a speeding ticket—"The speed limit is too slow."

If she is crabby—"She's got a burp in her." (A grandmother may still use this excuse for crabbiness even when the grandchild is 13 years old.)

If she spills her milk—"Somebody filled the glass too full."

If he kicks his doctor in the shins—"He wants a second opinion."

If she is ejected from the theater for throwing popcorn at the screen—"Well, no wonder, with the movies they make nowadays."

If he is picked up for littering from a car—"He can't stand an untidy car."

If she refuses to walk down the aisle when she is a flower girl—"She probably has a premonition that the marriage won't last."

It took a long time for most grandmothers to accept that their children weren't perfect. It takes even longer with their grandchildren.

Chapter 5

A Picture Is Worth a Thousand Oohs and Aahs

Grandmas have been known,
When paying a visit,
To show all their pictures,
Saying, "Aren't they exquisite?"

Grandmas love to show off pictures of their grandchildren. The hard part is coming up with a catchy line to secure the attention these pictures deserve. Here are some suggestions:

Say to your doctor, "I would like to show you my grandchild's picture so you can tell me what pediatrician you would recommend for him."

Say, "Oh, you knit? Let me show you this picture of my granddaughter in a sweater that I knit for her."

Ask the parking lot attendant, "Would you please hold my pictures while I search for my keys?"

Ask the checker at the supermarket, "Would you like to see a picture of the grandchildren who will be eating all these groceries?"

Ask the letter carrier, "Would you like to see a picture of the children who are sending me these letters?"

Say to the ticket-taker, "I don't have my senior citizen discount card with me, but these pictures of my grandchildren should prove my age."

If you're at a loss for an opener, one effective strategy is to arrange the pictures loosely in your billfold so they fall out and people have to help you pick them up.

Grandmas love to show off pictures of their grandchildren.

III
Don't Call Grandma at Exercise Class to Baby-sit

Chapter 6

Grandmothers Don't Need References

When you're baby-sittin',
The tot by whom you're smitten
Is apt to be a-spittin'
And make you feel like quittin'.

My mother warned me, "When you get a compliment from a boy, it means he is about to make sexual advances." I had to find out for myself that when a son or daughter gives a compliment, it may be leading to a request for baby-sitting.

Some parents don't even feel it's necessary to butter up the grandparent. They expect you to feel their call is "opportunity knocking." Thinking your life is empty without baby-sitting, they want to help fill the void.

Today's grandmother does not wish to give unlimited time to baby-sitting, but it is difficult to get out of when the recruiting campaign begins. When your children can't get in touch with you by phone, they will all but send a posse to track you down.

Don't be surprised if they embroider the truth when they try to get you to baby-sit. For instance, they might say, "We hated to ask the other grandma again," even though the other grandma has never baby-sat once.

"Will you just keep an eye on them for about an hour?" means keeping two eyes on them for a minimum of five hours.

Sometimes they say, "You can put him down for a nap after lunch," even though the child has been through with naps for a year.

Many grandmothers say, "I'll only baby-sit in a real emergency," thinking a real emergency comes along no more often than once a year. Wrong! It's amazing how many "real emergencies" come up:

"We're having the boss over for dinner."

"We have to go apartment hunting."

"We have to go to teachers' conferences."

"We're painting."

"We're wallpapering."

"We're playing in a tennis tournament."

"We need some time to ourselves."

Here are some tips for getting out of baby-sitting while maintaining your status as a beloved grandmother:

Collect brochures of motels where children can accompany parents free of charge.

If you see your daughter or daughter-in-law drive up and you think she wants to leave the kids, answer the door in your volunteer smock.

If the request is made by phone, say, "Just a second—I have to sneeze. There. Now what is it you want?"

If it's winter, say, "I have to keep turning the heat up and down because of my hot flashes and I'm afraid the baby will catch cold."

During the cold and flu season, say, "I'm on cold tablets and they make me drowsy."

During the month before Halloween, say, "I'm afraid they might find the trick-or-treat candy I bought and get sick."

Mention that you're planning to explain the facts of life while you have them. Your daughter may remember the terrible job you did with her and decide not to leave them.

If you don't feel like baby-sitting, use your imagination.

It's helpful to have a jarful of clever excuses to go to when you're stumped. Here are some proven winners:

"The dog chewed a leg off the baby bed."

"The cleaning lady threw out all the toys and story-books."

"I'm sorry, but I'm going away. In fact, they're out there now honking for me." (Go to a car accessories store and buy a horn to have by the phone, put a pillow over it, and honk it.)

"Sure. Bring them over. I was just cooking lunch: spinach and liver."

"I can't be disturbed now, I'm painting." (Don't let them know it's your fingernails.)

"I can't bring myself to take away work from someone who needs it."

"If I baby-sit any more, I'll have to get a license."

Even a grandmother who excels in making excuses will be talked into baby-sitting at times. For hours, she will be playing "Where's your mouth? Where's your nose? Where's your belly button?" and asking herself, "Where the heck are your parents?"

Here are a few suggestions to ease the task of baby-sitting:

Show up for baby-sitting wearing a pin that says, "TRAINEE" so they won't expect much.

Don't put on makeup. If you look pale, they might be a little more conscientious about getting home on time.

Parents won't dawdle if they know they are being timed.

Suggest playing "Let's see who can go the longest without making a sound."

Invent a game of Church, Temple, or Library.

Don't let them wear their "I LOVE MY GRANDMA" T-shirts. It makes it too hard to discipline them.

Pretend you are taking their picture, and spend a long time making them pose.

Have your grandchild do your exercises with you to sap a little of his energy.

Give the kids caramel apples so their mouths get stuck shut.

Don't look at the TV schedule. Knowing what programs you are giving up in favor of cartoons will make you feel bad.

Tell your grandchildren to look up "weeds" in the encyclopedia. Then, send them out to pick as many as they can.

When the parents walk out of the house, leaving the kids with you, say, "On your mark, get set, go," so the parents know they are being timed.

Have the children put on their coats at the exact time the parents said they would pick them up. Even if they are late, seeing the kids all ready to go home will lift your spirits.

Stretch your imagination and invent ideas that will cover all the babysitting challenges you may face. A few useful tactics perfected by other grandmothers are worth adding to your repertoire:

Rent a billboard to advertise for a sitter for your grandchildren.

Don't agree to baby-sit until you've heard the day's weather forecast and know the children can play outside.

Throw a Twinkie down the basement steps, and after the kids run down for it, slam the door shut.

Call the children's godparents. They have a responsibility, too.

Let's face it: Baby-sitting is a bona fide occupational hazard of being a grandmother. Unfortunately, you don't get workman's comp.

Rent a billboard to advertise for a sitter for your grandchildren.

Chapter 7

You Shouldn't Mace Your Grandchild out of the Living Room

Put up the plant,
Hide the vase,
Leash the dog,
Secure the place.

When your children leave home, you naturally look forward to having good furniture—finally! You think, "Now I can arrange everything for my own enjoyment."

But you will soon realize that this is just a fantasy. There is no time so short as the time between when your kids stop wrecking your furniture and your grandchildren start.

The trouble begins the first time your grandchild crawls. It's time, once again, to childproof your home.

Preparing for your grandchildren is extremely important. To guard against disasters to your grandchildren and your valuables:

Offer to baby-sit for a young mother in the neighborhood. Use her child as a guinea pig to find out where the perils exist in your home. Any normal child will run directly to a danger spot.

Safeguard your coffee table. Get rid of it, pad it, or attach a pulley that will hoist it to the ceiling.

Don't leave your mail lying around. Credit ratings have been ruined by toddlers doing away with bills.

Order out for food. Baby-sitting is a perfect excuse not to cook. You can say, "Emily will never trust me again if she burns herself on my stove."

Don't let them play dolls with your Hummels.

Make sure your keys are put away. It's not grandmotherly to frisk your grandchild every time he leaves your house.

A loose diaper can slow down a baby considerably.

Let him bang on a kettle, but not when it's full of hot soup.

Keep the telephone out of reach. But keep it in sight so you can threaten to phone the kids' parents if they're naughty.

Children can open childproof caps better than you can, so stay healthy and don't keep medicine around.

Fasten the baby's diaper loosely so she can't get around as fast.

Remember, though, that in the contest between the child and the childproofer, the childproofer will usually lose. And your cherished possessions will pay the price.

Chapter 8

My Favorite Number Is 98.6

A grandmother's hand on the forehead
May seem old-fashioned and sweet.
But in detecting a fever
It has a thermometer beat.

Grandchildren occasionally get sick. Usually, they are too sick to go to school but not sick enough for their mother to stay home from work and care for them. That's when Grandma gets an urgent phone call.

Beware of the sick child! Under normal circumstances, you may adore your grandchild and he may adore you back. But when he is sick, the Mutual Admiration Society disbands. You won't be able to do anything to please him, and he won't make life pleasant for you, either.

A sick child is not a delightful person, yet it is best not to tease him about the way he is acting. For instance, don't say, "Let me check—are you lying on a cocklebur?" Practice positive thinking, like reminding yourself that shaking down a thermometer is good for your arthritis.

It would be nice if there were some rule that accurately gauged the time of recovery—such as "fever before seven breaks before eleven"—but there isn't. You just have to wait and muster the best cribside manner you can.

It is best to make a contract with the child at the beginning: He will tell you the minute he starts to get better, if you don't ask him how he feels every five minutes.

The grandmother who says, "If you're sick enough to stay home, you're too sick to watch television" is a masochist. However, if the child has to stay in bed and doesn't have a television set in his room, don't try to carry the living room TV into his bedroom by yourself.

Get the medicine into the child as soon as possible. Don't wait for the pharmacy to deliver it. It will no doubt arrive after the parent gets home, and the child won't start to improve under your care. Ask a friend to pick it up for you.

Don't expect the child to take the medicine without a fight. If you can't disguise an onion so the child will eat it, how do you expect to slip icky medicine down her throat?

And don't expect to get anything done, other than care for the sick child. One grandmother tried exercising to an aerobics tape while caring for her sick grandson. But she could only get one "kick right" and one "kick left" done between requests from her patient. She called the walk to his room "cool-down time."

Follow these suggestions when caring for your sick grandchild:

Check his mouth before taking his temperature. It is hard to get chewing gum off a thermometer.

Pretend her doll has the same illness she has, and point out how good her doll is being.

Don't try to get a second opinion of his temperature from the Avon Lady or the Fuller Brush Man.

Tell her the dog or cat or hamster or goldfish will catch her cold if she doesn't put her hand over her mouth when she coughs or sneezes.

Realize that even if you bring the child up-to-date on your "soaps," he'll still insist on watching his favorite cartoons.

Don't be a chain temperature-taker.

Don't let him persuade you to have the sickbed transferred to his tree house.

You can't force fluids and not expect multiple "take me to the bathroom" requests.

Be sure you never tell your sick grandchild, "You think you're sick? I'm missing a 75-percent-off sale!"

The other side of the sick grandchild story is when the baby-sitter gets ill. One word of advice: If your grandchild's regular baby sitter is sick, tell the parents to get her the best doctor they can find and offer to pay for it. It's well worth it!

Don't even try to take his temperature while he's chewing gum.

Chapter 9

Don't Take Time to Smell the Roses If They're Made of Frosting

To tone up my stomach
Has long been my goal,
But my stomach's tone deaf,
So I need "girdle control."

From the moment your grandchildren learn to walk, they never stop moving during their waking hours. So if you ever hope to catch the little rascals, you'll have to get into shape.

It's true that slimming down is something a woman has to do for herself. But a grandmother can utilize grandchildren in her weight-loss project.

Wear your most revealing outfit in front of your grandchildren. One of them will probably say something cruel and give your program fresh motivation.

Have your grandchildren go through your magazines and rip out pictures of rich food and recipes for desserts.

When your grandchildren eat at your house, have them scrape their own plates so you won't be tempted to eat their leftovers.

Take your grandchildren out to eat. You will be so busy keeping them out of trouble that you won't have time to eat.

At the restaurant, order one child's portion and one adult's portion. Then, when the food comes, switch—you take the child's.

Eat with your grandchild's baby spoon.

For dessert, order coffee—not coffee ice cream.

Don't offer to hide the Halloween and Easter candy at your house.

Tell your grandchild, "If you love Grandma, don't offer her bites."

Exercise is very helpful in slimming down. Sometimes, though, you have to stretch your imagination to get your stretching done:

Taking care of your grandchildren's dog while they're away will give you plenty of exercise.

Instead of sitting in a chair and rocking your grandchild to sleep, walk the floor with him.

Oil the wheels on the stroller so you can jog as you push your grandchild.

Learn your grandson's paper route so you can take over when he's sick or on vacation.

Let your grandson borrow your car when he needs wheels. This ensures you'll do a lot of walking.

When your grandchildren are going on vacation, offer to take care of the dog. If you take him out when he wants to go, you will get exercise walking. If you don't take him out when he wants to go, you will get exercise scrubbing the carpet.

Avoid being too exercise conscious: Even though the bending takes inches off your waist, let your grandson pick up his own toys.

Chapter 10

Operation "Night, Night"

When he's finally tucked in bed
And you hear another peep,
It's only wishful thinking
That he's talking in his sleep.

"Well, I guess I'll hit the sack" is not likely to be uttered by a grandchild you're baby-sitting. In fact, a child's goal is just the opposite—to stay up forever. It's a conspiracy. Kids must trade bedtime excuses at nursery school.

If they say, "Just let me color one more picture," it will take longer than it took Michelangelo to paint the Sistine Chapel.

You'll get sleepy before your grandchildren do, but it is most important that you don't fall asleep while they are still awake. A good motto is, "Don't tire until you *can't see* the whites of their eyes."

Without putting it into words, they are telling you, "*I* decide when I go to bed." You can sing them your complete repertoire of lullabies five times, and they will be as wide awake as if they had drunk 10 cups of coffee.

Grandmothers try many ways of enforcing bedtime. They generally start with variations of a polite request:

"I would appreciate it very much if you would go to bed now."

"I will respect you more if you go to bed now."

Don't be fooled; your grandchild's goal is to stay up forever.

"Let's save that until tomorrow."

"Trust me—you'll feel much better tomorrow morning."

If the grandchildren don't respond to your polite requests, try a little creativity:

Change a nursery rhyme:

"Little Bo Peep

"Loved to sleep

"And so did her sheep."

Show them a picture of Goldilocks in the bed she found "just right."

Videotape a television station's sign-off and test pattern and play it at 7 p.m.

Ask "Do you want to go to bed at 6:30 or 7?" In fact, you can give four or five choices—all before 7, of course.

Tell them how well their cousins go to bed.

If they won't go to bed because they're afraid of the bogeyman, make yourself scarier than the bogeyman.

Or try this horror story: "The jails are full of kids who stayed up past their bedtime."

You can be sure that after you finally get them to bed, they will call you back into the bedroom or make unauthorized return trips to the living room, pouting, "I can't sleep with the lights on." There's also the classic line: "There's a monster under my bed."

The bedroom's distance from the living room makes no difference. Children either make themselves heard from their bedroom or reappear in the living room. You will probably get to the point where, when you hear the sound of footsteps, you hope it's a burglar.

The pressure of getting the grandchildren to go to bed and having them stay there can produce desperate acts. One grandmother took to watching TV without the sound on. Another grandmother refused to baby-sit again until her son got a squeaky floor board fixed.

Think long and hard before you rock a child to sleep. One grandmother said, "She cried when I finally put her in bed because I rocked her so long she had grown attached to me and I couldn't uproot her."

Re-bedding is an art in itself, requiring careful preparation:

If they call out, "I forgot to say my prayers," answer, "Just double them tomorrow night."

Put a "NO TRESPASSING" sign in the living room.

Unless you can hear their stomachs growling from the living room, don't feel obligated to get them anything to eat.

As a last resort, some grandmothers use threats: "You'd better be back in bed by the time I count to three or else." Unfortunately, a grandmother's "or else" isn't very scary.

IV
Look Before You Lip

Chapter 11

They Only Fear
Having You Interfere

My children are outstanding.
In their fields, they have gone far.
If they'd listened to their mother,
They'd be greater than they are.

It goes without saying that if your children followed your advice, they'd be much better off. Still, a grandmother should never expect to hear "Great idea!" or "Good tip!" when she makes a suggestion. It is obvious they do not wish to be better off. They want you to keep your recommendations to yourself.

Every grandmother I know makes a supreme effort not to interfere. The other day, I was talking to a friend whose daughter-in-law had just had a baby. She said they named her "Jennifer." I inquired what the middle name was, and she said, "I don't know. I didn't want to seem nosy."

No matter how badly you think your advice is needed, you must practice self-control. For example, don't ask in horror, "You're not going to let him take his 'blankie' to school, are you?"

Granted, it isn't easy to bite your tongue. You want to get at least one or two words in edgewise sometime. One grandmother suggested to her daughter-in-law, "I'll set a timer, and you just listen till it dings." For her birthday present, another grandma asked if she could make three suggestions.

Being prevented from speaking up is so frustrating that desperate acts come to mind—like driving into the power pole in front of their house to stop your grandchildren from spending all their time watching TV.

One grandmother's sad story is typical of bad experiences grandmothers have had in making recommendations for their children's children: "I brought some vitamins to their house, and they took the cotton from the bottle and stuffed it in their ears."

If your children ever did take any of your advice, it probably wouldn't work out anyway. For example, if you talked them into forcing your grandson to get a haircut, the temperature would drop to below zero and his ears would get frostbitten.

Here is some advice about not giving advice:

Have a cup of coffee handy so you can take a sip when you're about to speak.

If you do get as far as opening your mouth to tell them something, put your hand over it and pretend you are covering a yawn.

If your children don't believe in boots, meet your grandchild on the way to school and put some on him. Then meet him on the way home and take them from him.

Don't bother to take voice or diction lessons. They still won't listen to you.

Under no circumstances should you send the parents an anonymous letter.

Grandmothers want to give advice because they are concerned. But being *too concerned* is worse than being *unconcerned*. Here is a list of symptoms that will alert you to the fact that you worry too much. Do you . . .

Pull the main fuse when your grandchildren visit so they won't get shocks?

Worry about your grandchild getting housemaid's knee because he does too much crawling?

Buy them fluorescent pajamas in case they sleepwalk outside?

Go "trick or treating" with the kids to hold up their long costumes so they don't trip on porch steps?

Don't go trick or treating with your grandchild; stay home and enjoy some candy before it's all gone.

Yell "Close your eyes!" when their picture is being taken because of the flash?

Forbid them to go on morning field trips to the arboretum because their feet will get wet from the dew on the grass?

Put a net under their bunk bed?

Try to bribe the driving examiner to flunk your grandchildren?

Of course, one of a grandmother's primary duties is to worry about her grandchildren. If you don't, people will think you're not doing your job.

Chapter 12

It's Nice to Have an "In" with Your In-Law

By your grandchild you are cherished.
Your words are heard with awe.
But to your grandchild's parent,
You're just a mother-in-law.

Relationships between grandmothers and in-laws are often difficult. There is frequently an underlying feeling of mistrust. One sweet little grandmother told me that her daughter-in-law had her tested for drugs before she could baby-sit.

A daughter-in-law is not afraid of incurring her mother-in-law's wrath by naming her son "Kyle" and breaking a chain of eight generations of first sons named "William."

"My daughter-in-law won't let me kiss an 'owie' for fear I'll make them hypochondriacs," a grandmother disclosed. I've even heard of a daughter-in-law who accused the grandmother of being a curiosity seeker when she asked if the baby had a tooth yet.

Discord between grandmothers and in-laws is more easily understood when you consider the diverse backgrounds from which couples come. For example, SHE comes from a family that sends the child to school as soon as possible; HE comes from a home convinced that if you send her a year later, she'll do better. HER dinners were salads; HIS, meat and potatoes.

Relationships between grandmas and in-laws are often difficult.

HER parents gave big allowances; HIS said, "You can keep half the money you find between the cushions."

Sometimes a daughter-in-law will do anything to declare her mother the *favorite* grandmother. One such villainess let her child wear a T-shirt saying "MY HEART BELONGS TO GRANDMA" only in front of *her* mother. When her husband asked her to put it on when going to *his* mother's home, she refused, saying she didn't want her child to be a phony.

Nonetheless, with a little work, you can have a happy relationship with your in-laws.

Let them visit you. "Home court advantage" also works for grandmothers.

Be satisfied if they use the other grandma's name for the baby's first name and yours for the baby's middle name.

Don't say, "Jennifer's shoelace is untied," just tie it. Very few daughters-in-law are ornery enough to untie it again.

If they decide to go to the other grandma's for Christmas, don't take offense. Just say you're planning to spend Christmas in Hawaii.

To encourage them to bring your grandchildren to visit you, order cable TV, or buy a VCR, a compact disc player, and some video games.

Stand strong against the forces of the in-laws. For instance, you might say, "I know you want Joshua to be a vegetarian, Linda, but I'm giving him meat because I happen to know he inherited his father's taste buds."

But no matter how bitter the feelings are between you and the in-laws, remember this: It is just as hard to resist the grandchild peering up at you with the in-law's brown eyes as with your family's blue eyes.

Chapter 13

"But My
Other Grandma . . . "

The other grandma may be great.
There's croquet on her terrace.
If you don't want to break my heart,
You'd better not compare us.

It is demoralizing to have a grandchild point out how the "other Grandma" outshines you. The little devil's a master at making statements that are guaranteed to produce jealousy:

"My other Grandma turns off her 'soaps' when I come over."

"My other Grandma doesn't make my birthday cake from a mix."

"My other Grandma doesn't read me stories—she makes them up."

"My other Grandma doesn't talk on the phone when I'm there."

"My other Grandma never calls me the wrong name."

"My other Grandma never takes me across the street on the 'NO WALK' light."

"My other Grandma always lets me go into the toy department."

"My other Grandma can help me with my math."

"My other Grandma saves all of my drawings."

"My other Grandma always checks the expiration date on the milk."

"My other Grandma never gives me clothes for presents."

"My other Grandma is never in her bathrobe in the daytime."

"My other Grandma never drives this fast when she's taking me home."

Unfortunately, the other grandma is usually unavailable when a baby-sitter is needed.

The little tykes are masters at producing jealousy.

Chapter 14

Thank God for Alexander Graham Bell and the Wright Brothers

When you send a letter,
Send a photo, too,
So when you pay a visit,
They'll know it's really you.

Do you feel that grandmothers who talk about their grandchildren stopping in after school are braggarts? Then you are a long-distance grandmother.

There are many drawbacks to living far away from your grandchildren:

You can't kiss an "owie" over the telephone.

You get so lonesome for them you are apt to cry if someone says words like "pablum" or "pediatrician."

When you visit them there's a good chance your bedroom was closed off and won't get warm until you're ready to go home.

And, by the time your suitcase is unpacked and your clothes are hung up, you'll feel you've overstayed.

Although having your grandchildren live out of town is not the best situation, you can learn to accept the role of the long-distance grandmother:

Don't cry while addressing their packages. Your tears will smudge the address.

Call them at a time when they are most likely to be crabby (such as Sunday evening when they are depressed about going back to school). It will kill your desire to be with them.

Suggest they go into acting and do commercials so you can see them on TV.

When visiting the grandchildren, you might just freeze to death if you're not prepared.

Have them just tell you the bad things that are happening in their lives. You will be happy you aren't on the scene.

Don't listen to the national weather report and call them when you think they should carry an umbrella.

You can refuse to talk to all their little friends on the phone without feeling guilty if the friends have grandparents of their own.

Don't send your children subscriptions to your local newspaper. Your grandchildren might get a job from the want ads and move in with you.

One point to keep in mind when you visit: It isn't grandmotherly to put a "DO NOT DISTURB" sign on your bedroom door.

V
Don't Be a Closet Advice-Giver

Chapter 15

Don't Put Your Elbows on the Table or into Anyone Else's Ribs

If he spills,
It won't hurt
When he's wearing
A Hawaiian shirt.

Many children today have poor table manners. It's miserable to get pitying glances from strangers when you are out with your grandchildren. It's even worse to get them from friends.

Children do many things that are incompatible with eating in mixed company—that is, any meal with children and adults. To help give your grandchilden social graces, have them memorize this list of "don'ts":

"Don't butter the bottom of the bowl so you can slide it down the table."

"Don't form obscene words with your string beans."

"Don't use the fork to clean your fingernails."

"Don't pick the onions out of the casserole."

"Don't make a sandwich out of the casserole."

"Don't use a water glass for a fingerbowl—especially not your sister's water glass."

"Don't wipe the spots off the silverware with a piece of bread."

"Don't sing with your mouth full."

"Don't hold up a finger for the others to use as an onion ring toss."

"Don't throw pits at your brothers and sisters—or try to plant them in someone's chocolate pudding."

Don't be disappointed if your cleverest lines don't work.

Nutrition, like manners, is also incompatible with childhood. They say "icky" and you say "picky." Most children do not by nature eat the way they should. When asked, "How do you want your eggs?" one little boy replied, "In chocolate cake."

Getting milk down their throats is a struggle, too. Usually, a drop of milk in a glass and "When!" are simultaneous.

Children are always in a hurry. A little boy's hands don't have time to dry from their before-meal washing before he asks to be excused from the table. He takes one bite of breakfast and asks, "What's for lunch?"

Nonetheless, it is your duty to try to instill proper eating habits:

> Be firm when your grandchild balks at eating. Say, "Eat that cottage cheese, or you will sit here until the lettuce under it turns brown!" (But don't say, "If you eat carrots, you can see better and it will be easier to cheat on tests.")

> Give him a cloth napkin instead of a paper one, so he can't wad food up in it and throw it away.

> Tell him he can't lick the whipped cream beaters if he doesn't lick the mashed potato beaters.

> The right atmosphere can contribute to a more pleasant meal. For instance, around Christmas, it helps to play "Santa Claus Is Coming to Town" as dinner music.

Don't expect that all your clever ideas will pan out. It doesn't help to serve brussels sprouts in banana split dishes or to cover them with brandy and serve them as a flaming dessert. Saying "Brussel sprouts were the official vegetable of the Olympics" won't do the trick, either. Your grandchild still won't eat them.

Chapter 16

Too Many Cooks Spoil the Looks of Grandma's Kitchen

When the timer dings,
Her cookies are done.
But cleaning up the mess
Won't be as much fun.

Worse for any young woman than not having a dowry is going into marriage without cooking lessons from her grandmother.

Grandmotherly culinary instruction is a must, but don't be misled by the picture of the smiling woman on the cover of the Junior Cookbook. At seven or eight, your granddaughter will not have had any home economics courses, and there may be many unpleasant occurrences.

Here's what you can expect:

You will have to play 52 pick-up with the cinnamon candies.

She will either eat the cookie dough balls or juggle them.

All the cards in your recipe file will become permanently stuck together.

There will be a stonelike batter on the timer.

The gingerbread men will be headless, armless, and legless by the time they are baked.

Spills on the floor will be wiped up with your best white dish towel.

When the dough's in the oven, your grandchild will wander into the living room and wipe her sticky hands on the sofa.

To be assured of the best outcome in this venture, it is important to make sure your grandchild is not too young to learn to cook. Keep her out of the kitchen by any means if . . .

She asks if she can use the cooking utensils in her sandbox.

She runs her cars through the sugar and flour.

The object of your cooking lesson is to have your granddaughter be able to cook by herself. But it will always be difficult not to be a "backseat baker" when you are with her.

Here are some preventive measures worth taking:

Warn her that she won't get the number of cookies stated on the recipe if she doesn't stop tasting the cookie dough.

Keep a seltzer bottle in your apron pocket to put out fires.

Have plenty of pan scrubbers on hand, because a child cannot differentiate between "crisp" and "burned."

Practice saying "Yummy" so that no matter how awful the cookies turn out, you can compliment her.

If you have started cooking lessons and find it is not your cup of tea, here are a few ways you can get off the hook:

Put a TV in the kitchen. She may get interested in a program and stop helping you.

Send her to the store for a "missing ingredient," and tell her to play video games with the change.

Ask, "Why don't you just draw pictures of cakes, pies, and cookies?"

Put the chairs up on top of the table—as if the kitchen is closed.

No matter how severely your patience is tried, don't prolong the agony by insisting she wash the dishes. If you want *something* to be cleaned, run a bath for *her*.

Chapter 17

Keep Your Nose to the Grindstone and Your Eyes on the Sidewalk for Money

If you don't want them
To live in squalor,
Teach them the value
Of a dollar.

No one seems to take on the responsibility for teaching children the value of a dollar anymore. What better person to do it than a grandmother who lives on a fixed income and has learned the hard way?

To instill the virtue of frugality:

Suggest that it's better to shop in the generic aisles, because all those bright colors on brand name products are hard on the eyes.

Tell children, "You're more likely to find a book you'll enjoy at the library. Besides, if you don't like it, you can always bring it back."

Teach them games that will make standing in line at sales more fun.

Rationalize that their older brothers and sisters will feel bad if they don't wear their hand-me-downs.

Explain that a mutt makes a more obedient pet than a pedigreed dog.

Tell them the ducks are happier if you make duck sounds than if you throw them popcorn.

Saving money is a lot easier for your grandchildren if you show the way:

Teach your grandchild to say, "I gave at school," so

You'll have enough bread and butter for a week if you bring a big doggie bag.

later on he'll be comfortable saying, "I gave at the office."

Suggest that your granddaughter always carry a big purse, in case she goes someplace where they're giving out samples.

Tell the children that when they throw pennies in a fountain, some poor person will get wet and catch cold fishing them out.

Teach them to ask "Does it cost extra?" when a waiter asks if they want bleu cheese or salad dressing. And remind them to bring home the uneaten bread, rolls, crackers, and butter in a doggy bag. (But they should leave the wicker bread basket on the table.)

Tell them to always order "the works," because they'll get more for their money.

At a motel, warn them never to ask directions from anyone in uniform—they'll expect a tip.

You can give gifts that teach the value of a dollar:

Give them crisp new dollar bills so they will be more likely to save them.

Give them piggybanks that make it impossible to get the money out. Make sure the bank is so cute they won't want to break it.

Give them some tapes of old Jack Benny shows.

Perhaps the best way to get thrift into their blood is to inscribe the idea indelibly in their minds. Repeat the advertising slogan of your local savings bank. Or, better yet, teach them your motto: "If it isn't on sale, I don't really need it."

Chapter 18

Work Is a
Four-Letter Word

The only time they want to know
What it was like many years ago,
Is when you hand them rake or hoe
Or tell them to get out and mow.

If you want to make your grandchildren more familiar with the work ethic, hire them to do chores for you.

You should rationalize, however, that having the work done *fast* and *well* is expecting too much. Grandchildren always love to play in water, but when you add soap and a scrub brush, it's another story.

To have a remote chance of getting any work done at all, make sure your grandchild is old enough to work. Your grandchild is too young for labor if . . .

He rakes the leaves into a pile and then jumps in.

You hand her a broom and she plays "horsey" with it.

Grandmas are known softies when it comes to having their grandchildren work for them. In most cases, they have to sit on their hands to keep from helping. A grandmother is not an effective employer if . . .

After the grandchild walks over to her house, she worries that he is too tired to work.

Kids hanging around your refrigerator are probably not reading your list of chores.

She pays her grandchild for shoveling the snow, even though it has melted by the time he arrives.

She pays him for mowing the lawn, even if the lawn-mower runs out of gas before the job is finished.

She can't bear the thought of her grandchild getting callouses.

There are certain things you can expect when you have your grandchildren work for you:

Your telephone will ring off the hook, because your grandchild will give out your number to all her friends so she won't miss any calls.

She'll show up in midafternoon, explaining, "I overslept, Grandma."

Your grandchildren will complain that your house is too big, even though in the past they always complained that it was too small.

You'll hear "I'm done, Grandma!" several times before you can spot any progress.

When your grandchildren are in your service, follow these rules:

Don't give a little one part of an old blanket to clean with. She may start sucking her thumb and take a nap.

Don't just say, "Dust." If you don't mention each item you expect to be dusted, only the coffee table in front of the TV set will get cleaned.

If they're wearing earphones, write down your instructions and hold them directly in front of their eyes.

Don't hang their list of chores on the refrigerator. Each time they go to see what to do next, they'll open the door and get something to eat.

Don't give your grandson jobs different from those you give your granddaughter. They'll call you sexist.

If they bring a good book for you to read when they come, take the clue and don't supervise them as they work.

Be nice to them so they won't tell their mother how dirty your house is.

When you think about it, why should your grandchildren try to impress you by working hard? How valuable is a reference from your grandmother?

Chapter 19

Not Now, Honey—
I've Got a Headache

The story of
The birds and bees
Should not be learned
At Grandma's knees.

A grandmother is happy to hand a child over to the mother when the child asks, "Where did I come from?" But sometimes the grandmother is put on the spot and there's no one else to turn to.

Although the sexual revolution is a fact of life now, most grandmothers grew up before the first shot was fired. It is hard to know which is more difficult for a grandmother to understand—the new math or the new sex.

You probably shouldn't try to impart the facts of life if . . .

You turn off the television when you are with your grandchild and a commercial for a "personal-care product" comes on.

You leave the room when your granddaughter walks in wearing a bikini—and she's only 8.

You won't take your grandchild and your dog for a walk at the same time.

You have no bear-skin rug pictures in your photo album.

There's an emphasis today on making sure a child's sexual inquisitiveness is met with a complete and accurate response. For instance, if a child asks, "Why is this called a love seat?" he gets all the facts of life. Experts counsel that when the child poses a sex question, he should be answered that very second.

If your grandchildren ask you a question about sex:

Pretend you don't hear it.

Say, "Here's a pen—write to Dr. Ruth."

Use words of three syllables or more—like "chromosomes"—so they'll be bored and won't ask you anything again.

Ask him, "Where do you think you came from?"

Sometimes grandmotherly advice can backfire.

Counter with, "Instead of answering that, would you be satisfied if I told you my age and weight?"

Tell them to ask their other grandma.

Feign a memory lapse and say, "I don't remember."

Say, "If I tell you now, you'll be bored when you get to biology class."

Say, "Keep watching *Jeopardy*—they'll probably answer your question.

Don't tell your granddaughter, "All you need to know when you go out on a date is the word 'No.' " He could ask, "Do you think it's wrong to have sex on the first date?"

Probably the best answer came from my grandmother: She shrugged her shoulders and said, "Ya' got me!"

Chapter 20

Turn on the Educational Channel During the Baby's Feeding

Changing, feeding, bathing,
Putting cotton balls in jars—
I'd rather help the father
Pass out the cigars.

Many women get their first taste of grandmothering by helping a daughter or daughter-in-law when a new grandchild is born. Although this may sound simple enough, be forewarned. It's a lot more difficult than it sounds.

As one grandmother put it, "When I arrived at their home, the baby had colic and the mother insisted it was because I had spoiled him in the car on the way home from the hospital."

Her narrative continued: "The baby was fed on demand, and so was the rest of the family. He was so fussy, I picked up threads and lint off the floor because I didn't want to vacuum and wake him. To make matters worse, the baby's brother was always 'making it snow' with talcum powder."

Visitors constantly said to the other child, "The baby is so lucky to have you for a brother." Never once did anyone say, "The baby is so lucky to have you for a grandmother."

You know sibling rivalry has reared its ugly head when he wants the baby to sleep in the basement — right next to Spot.

It's hard to get any fun out of the hectic first week at home with a new baby. And if there is a child already in the home, a grandmother's heart goes out to him.

Parents often don't realize how much bringing a baby home upsets the other child; it's a problem that merits serious thought. Parents should try to soften the blow. For instance, if they take a cab home from the hospital—Mom and Dad could walk in first with a gift for the older sibling and the cabdriver could follow, carrying the baby.

The first child usually thinks that he's been replaced. He feels angry and wants revenge. Sometimes he tries to take it out on his grandmother by tattling "Grandma's wasting the milk on her arm" when you're testing the bottle.

A grandmother should know if the first child is jealous when these tell-tale signs appear:

He wants the baby to be kept in a box in the basement, just like the new puppy.

Her idea of entertaining the baby is snapping rubber bands at him.

When asked to pose with the new baby, he sits on her.

She tries to convince you to put the baby's crib in the treehouse.

Instead of bouncing a ball, he tries to bounce the baby.

To help out in this situation, you might try to con the first child with this line: "The baby is crying because he isn't old enough to play with you." But you might also consider buying a bulletproof vest for the baby, just in case.

Older siblings are not the only ones whose lives are complicated by a new baby. Grandma's life will be affected, too. Generations of first children have fallen for that one. To make the time you actually spend caring for a new grandchild as easy as possible:

Wear running shoes, so you can catch the phone on the first ring and greet visitors before they ring the doorbell.

Bring along wrinkleproof skirts and slacks, as the baby's brother or sister will always be sitting on your lap.

Don't stare at the mobile over the baby's crib. It can put you to sleep.

Don't attempt to give the mother baby-care advice via the three-year-old. It doesn't work.

If possible, try to limit your involvement with a new baby to starting a bank account for college.

VI
Taking Tantrums on the Road

Chapter 21

And a Side Order of Tranquilizers, Please

As soon as they've ordered,
And the waitress is gone,
You're bound to wonder,
"What's taking so long?"

I would buy stock in any restaurant chain that caters to people eating out with children. It would provide huge bibs, wipe-up rags, garbage bags, toys for the children, and presents for the adults who brought them. There would be only one meal on the menu and one choice of drink.

Children do not just walk into a restaurant, sit down, order and eat. They race ahead and spin on the counter stools, run and slide, tip over chairs, spill beverages, and whine. Nonetheless, you have to sit there with them. You can't say, "Let's split up," as you walk through the door.

Instead, you must learn to handle the situation. Learn to recognize these clues that the meal is not going to go well:

The waitress tells you her name, and the kids make fun of it.

They make paper airplanes out of all the napkins in the napkin dispenser.

They use the pen provided for the placemat game to scribble on the menu.

One child brags that he is old enough to use a fork and then proceeds to stab his brother.

When the waitress asks, "What would you like?" they say, "Guess!"

There isn't a videotape you can buy or rent showing a child how to behave properly in a restaurant, so you should list the "no-nos" in advance:

Don't check the coin-return while someone is using the pay phone.

Don't take tips off the table, unless you're planning to clear and wash the dishes.

Don't "save room for dessert" by not touching one bite of your main course.

Wouldn't it be great if you could drop the kids off at a restaurant and come back when they're finished?

If you're uncertain about where to take your grandchildren to eat, here are a few suggestions:

Some restaurants have aquariums or exotic birds. This will entertain the children for up to five minutes.

Pick a noisy place to eat to drown out your grandchildren's racket. A bowling alley is a perfect spot.

Go to a restaurant with loud music. If there is a jukebox, play it.

Don't go to a restaurant that has the menu pasted on the wall. The kids will keep reading it and changing their minds.

Don't go to a restaurant where there is a football or basketball game on TV. Your husband will watch that instead of help put on bibs, wipe up spills, and stop food fights.

Go to a restaurant in a department store that has a Santa Claus. They will be less apt to misbehave with Santa nearby.

You might wonder if you should take them out for lunch or for dinner. Children are more tired in the evening and apt to be crabby, but the muted lights restaurants have at night go a long way to cover up poor etiquette.

Want to make eating out with your grandchildren more enjoyable?

Before you leave the house, check your liability insurance to see if it covers damage to property caused by grandchildren.

Park far away from the restaurant. A hike of several blocks will sap the children's energy.

Before you go in, buy a newspaper from the dispenser outside. If the kids get really bad, you can hide behind it.

Don't choose seating based on smoking preference. Instead go into the section of the restaurant with the most children. Your grandchildren won't be so noticeable.

Tell the waitress you are a restaurant critic.

If a free glass is given, don't accept it. It always gets broken before you get home.

Tell the children Ronald McDonald is a bouncer.

Don't bring along a coupon. They will fight over who is going to present it.

Have them eat with their jackets on. They will be more restricted in their movements.

If you have arthritic fingers, when the waitress asks how the child wants his hamburger or steak, say, "Cut up."

Elbows on the table can be overlooked, but feet on the table should be knocked off.

When one child has to go to the restroom, don't ask the couple at the next table to watch the others while you take him.

Make your grandchildren bounty hunters. Pay them for any fly or bug they catch.

Remember that the Heimlich maneuver doesn't work on food placed in the nose.

If your waitress tells you they just ran out of the last piece of pie, don't go over to the person who got it and try to buy it from him for your grandchild.

Sit between the children. It cuts down on hitting and pinching.

Don't bawl them out with your mouth full.

Forget about having the kids order something nutritious. It is hard enough to get them to choose anything—so don't argue with them when they finally make a decision.

Tell them that this is the restaurant where the Sesame Street characters eat and that one of them may come through the door at any minute.

Maybe you have grandchildren who are just not acceptable restaurant patrons under any circumstances. Indications

You know you're in trouble when you are snubbed by your waitress.

that you should eat out only in your own backyard are when . . .

Two waitresses flip a coin and the loser walks over to your table.

You ask the waitress what she suggests and she says, "The restaurant next door."

A relief waitress is brought in.

The manager says, "Your meal is on the house—if you promise not to come back."

If you feel embarrassed by your grandchildren's misbehavior, here's what to do:

Leave the money with the check, and don't wait for the change.

Use the restaurant's intercom to apologize to the other diners.

Tip more than 75 percent.

It is expensive to take your grandchildren to a restaurant, so it's important that you learn from the experience. When you get home, write down the name of the restaurant and a description of how your grandchildren behaved. If they were just a step away from getting arrested for disturbing the peace, make sure you don't go there again.

Chapter 22

Grandparents' Day Comes Before Bridge Club

When you visit her classroom,
Your heart will swell with pride,
But when you're at the playground,
Don't go down the slide!

There is nothing more exciting than receiving a grand-child-written invitation to attend a school program planned just for you. I'm referring to Grandparents' Day, an annual event in many elementary schools.

It really is a day to enjoy. Savor it. You should realize your grandchild didn't have to invite you. He could have said you were dead. Also, understand that in a few years, he won't be this proud of taking your hand and leading you along in front of his peers.

Be forewarned that the day may not be a pure delight. Many things can happen to temper your pleasure:

Your pantyhose could run from sitting down that low.

You could see the sweater you knit for him in the "Lost and Found."

Your back could go out getting a drink at the children's water fountain.

Your grandchild could whisper to his friend, "Pet Day is more fun."

The tissue paper carnation she made for you could clash with your dress.

Your grandchild could ask to use your dentures for "Show and Tell."

Consider these rules to help make the event a success.

Don't patronize the "other grandmother" by letting her go ahead of you in the punch line because she looks older than you.

Don't offer the teacher a better punch recipe.

Don't ask the school nurse questions about your health.

Your day in school may not be a pure delight.

Don't be too proud to dip the hard cookies into your coffee or punch.

Don't ask the teacher if you can sit in her chair.

Don't walk into the teachers' lounge to get away from feeling like you're in the "Land of the Munchkins."

The glow of attending Grandparents' Day lingers for a long time. It's heady stuff to have your grandson walk you down to the boiler room and introduce you to the custodian.

Chapter 23

The Computer Is Down and Being Sat On

When you bring them to the office
After you get hired,
Demand their best behavior,
Or you just might get fired.

It is natural for you to want the people you work with to admire your grandchildren. However, when brought to his grandmother's work place, the average child will not politely shake hands with people and stand quietly by Grandma's side.

Here are a few case histories of children whose proud grandmothers had them visit during office hours:

Jessica M. had a tantrum because her grandmother wouldn't paint her fingernails with typewriter correction fluid.

Jason L. caused the president of a company to say through clenched teeth, "You can't play Pac Man on our microcomputer's general ledger program!"

Eric S. took the money that had been collected for someone's wedding.

David L. did a somersault by the water cooler and knocked it over.

Don't let your grandchild visit the teachers' lounge.

Jennifer Y. visited the school where her grandmother taught and erased the next day's assignment from the blackboard.

Colin F. went with his grandmother into the employee's lounge and told his grandmother's boss, who was smoking, "Only stupid people smoke."

Amy T. told everyone that her grandma was really 62 but regularly gave her age as 55.

Sammy R. made 150 pictures of his hand on the copier.

If, despite these examples, you still can't resist the urge to show your grandchildren off, here are a few suggestions for the visit:

Give the children pieces of paper and tell them to design a new letterhead for the office.

Have them make a jump rope by linking paper clips together.

Call every office in the building to see if anyone needs any pencils sharpened.

Send the kids out to help the groundskeeper.

Definitely don't bring your grandchildren if your employer deducts breakage from your check.

And don't tell them Grandma will jump out the window if they don't behave. They won't.

There are some advantages to having your grandchildren visit you at work (other than getting a break from the normal office routine):

You will understand why the boss hates clock-watchers, because you'll hate the people who keep watching the clock until your grandchildren leave.

You will provide a little office gossip. Co-workers will be clucking their tongues for a long time afterward, saying, "Did you see those kids?!"

Perhaps you can earn some overtime cleaning up after your grandchildren.

But don't try to excuse what they did by saying such things as "If that file cabinet had been bolted to the floor like it should have been, Michael wouldn't have tipped it over."

After their visit, make sure you take all the pictures of your grandchildren off your desk. You don't want to unnecessarily remind your co-workers of your darling grandchildren.

Chapter 24

Don't Whimper on the Roller Coaster

Being stuck on
A ferris wheel
Doesn't have
A lot of appeal.

You have to really love your grandchildren to take them to an amusement park.

Touring the midway can be harmful to your health. When kids go where there are rides, cotton candy, hot dogs, and concessions with prizes, they don't want to go home. And, while all men are created equal, grandmothers have corns, bunions, and callouses and grandchildren don't.

Sore feet are a minor difficulty. The real problem is how to avoid the scary rides. Though advertisements for amusement parks never show grandmothers on the roller coaster, somehow, a grandchild expects his grandmother to ride it with him.

When he begs you to go on "The Volcano" or "The Death-dealing Destroyer," your sanity—which you lost momentarily when you agreed to this excursion—will return. "Entrust my life to that horrible contraption? No way!" you think. But it isn't easy to get out of going.

You will hear a variety of arguments:

"If anything goes wrong, Grandma, they'll give you your money back."

"You really get your money's worth, because it's a long ride."

"You will be my favorite grandmother if you go." (A most persuasive argument.)

It's important to be firm in your refusal to risk life and limb on those rides. A grandson does not feel the same about a grandmother who screams and buries her head in his lap.

To get out of going on a wild ride, tell your grandchild:

If you go, too, there will be no one to wave to him from the ground.

His friends will be more impressed with his courage if he goes on the ride alone.

And if a sign says, "Children Must be Accompanied by an Adult," say you don't have your birth certificate with you to prove your age.

Some rides are better left unridden.

But, no matter how desperate you may be, don't wreck your credibility by saying, "Get on and I'll join you later."

A grandmother at an amusement park needs all the help she can get, and then some. Follow these tips to stay out of trouble:

Have the children eat caramel apples and then tell them to hold hands so they don't get lost—they won't be *able* to let go.

Tell them to forget about ordering jumbo-size because Grandma's bank account is not jumbo-size.

Forbid grandchildren to play any game where the prize is goldfish. It's the one game they'll probably win.

Tell your grandson if he keeps throwing baseballs at milk bottles, he will wreck his arm for Little League.

One final hint: Think as positive as you can:

If they spill their drinks, think, "Good! Now we won't have to stand in the restroom line."

If you have long waits in line, think, "It's better to be safe and sound on the ground."

If the grandchildren get lost, remember, "While they're lost, they can't ask me for money."

Chapter 25

Wish They Were There

Remember,
When the travel bug bites,
You're better off
Without the mites.

When you are planning to take grandchildren along on a trip, delightful images appear in your mind: Excited children, who take turns sitting next to the window and pointing out sights such as sheep grazing or a new colt with its mother. Wide-eyed children, who at times cry out, "Look! A historical marker one-half mile ahead on the left!" Well-mannered children, who, should they on a rare occasion disagree, just don't talk to each other for a few miles. Happy children, who sing together like the Osmond family.

And you picture how everything will work out just right. You arrive at concession stands when there are only two people ahead of you in line. Everyone will acquire beautiful tans without getting one inch of sunburn.

Only when you stop for meals will they feel the need to go to the bathroom. All the souvenirs they purchase will fit nicely into their suitcases and each child—even a Zachary or an Imogene—will find his or her initial on a souvenir keychain.

The kids will pose for pictures smiling with their arms around one another. You, the navigator, will furnish directions to the driver so well you will get to every destination perfectly without having to circle one block.

From the back seat the kids will point out anything but the beauties of nature.

Finally, the allowance their parents gave them will last the whole trip and there will be enough left over to buy you flowers in appreciation of your taking them on vacation.

But think long and hard before taking your grandchildren with you on a trip. Things usually don't work out the way you'd hoped. For example, looking at animals along the way will consist mainly of trying to identify what poor creature has been squished on the highway. From the back seat, the kids will point out your arthritis bumps and their grandfather's baldness, but never the beauties of nature. "Pullovers" are not for sightseeing, but for disciplining. And the pillows you brought along will not be used for napping, but for throwing.

The highlight of the trip will be the discovery that the motel has an erotic movie channel. The low point will be your forbidding them to watch it.

A good substitute for taking your grandchildren on a trip is to make them *feel* like they're traveling without leaving your home town.

Buy them all sunglasses. When you take them to Sunday

school, take different routes to get there. Get out the city map and let them find your destination. While getting the car serviced, suggest they use the gas station restroom. Take them to a rummage sale and call it the Farmer's Market.

Better yet, make the children beg you to stay home. Order them gifts by mail so they will want to be home when they arrive. If they're teen-agers, tell them you heard that some interesting kids of the opposite sex are about to move into their neighborhood.

However, if your fantasy of the trip obscures reality and you do take off, here are some things you ought to know:

> It is cheaper to carry packed lunches than to eat in restaurants, but brown bagging it brings the danger of bags being popped in the car.

> Doubling up in the motel saves money, but it's not fun. All night, you will hear complaints like "Grandpa's snoring so loud I can't sleep" and "Jason's toenail cut me."

> Pointing out a water tower will either make them thirsty or have to go to the bathroom.

> Kids get carsick and grandparents get kidsick.

> A car doesn't have a basement or porch for getting away from the fray.

> Don't take a hard-cover journal to record your travels. It will be too tempting to reach into the back seat and hit the children with it.

> The Gideon Bible at the motel will have a passage to sustain you.

Next time *you* go on a trip alone, don't forget to bring back plenty of souvenirs for the grandchildren. Whatever the gifts cost you, it's a lot less expensive and exhausting than bringing your grandchildren along.

VII
I'm Afraid of Heights — My Grandchildren Are Getting Tall

Chapter 26

From "Gitchee Gitchee" to Gucci

They loved to talk
When they were small.
Now they hurry,
So they can play ball.

The missing front teeth have come in and are covered with metal. Lying-on-the-floor tantrums have been replaced by slamming-door tantrums. The spelling of their names is changed. Boy George and Madonna have replaced Kermit the Frog and Miss Piggy. You can't sing them lullabies because their ears are covered by earphones. They have gone from comic books to *Rolling Stone*. They duck in the car because they don't want to be seen with anyone driving the speed limit. They never take you to their room anymore to show you anything because it is such a mess.

To survive the teen-age years, you must learn not to become upset by the multiple piercings of the ears, the outlandish hair styles, or the sullenness. But it's not easy to keep cool when your grandchildren are trying their best to shock you. You just have to think about what they're doing in a different way:

Think of "surly" as "colicky."

Tell yourself they are still playing "dress up."

Call their home often. You will probably be breaking up a fight between your grandchild and his parents.

Don't ever buy them anything at a discount store.

Subscribe to a teen-age magazine to study their fashions, hair styles, and vocabulary.

Don't kiss the cut your grandson gets from shaving.

When he asks if his rock band can practice at your house, try to think of it as being like the time he banged on your pans with a spoon.

When your granddaughter picks up the wine list at the restaurant, don't snatch it away from her.

It's hard to be cool when they're trying to shock you.

Write letters to your sons and daughters. Trying to get through to them with teenagers on the phone can be very frustrating.

Don't say, "I'll keep looking for your other earring." They only wear one.

Tell yourself fluorescent hair will make them safer when they're out at night.

Give the kids money instead of gifts. Don't kill their love for you by picking out a present for them.

Best of all, look at pictures of your own children when they were young to remind yourself that even the worst teenagers eventually become acceptable adults.

Chapter 27

I Love My Grandson, But I Owe Something to My Car, Too

"He's driving too slow"
Is ne'er a complaint.
The speed limit sign
Is a waste of good paint.

When your grandson gets his temporary driver's license, he has to have someone take him out to get driving experience, and you are very apt to be that "someone."

Fifteen-year-olds never drive according to the motto "Easy does it." The only time they approach a reasonable and prudent speed is when driving through a carwash.

Gone are the days of practicing on untraveled country roads. Your grandson will insist on driving on the freeway at top speeds. And he won't hear your directions over the blaring radio. Should he ever have an accident, your daughter-in-law will blame it on what you taught him. Grandmothers who haven't smoked for 30 years have been known to start again from the pressure.

One of the biggest problems is in your mind. Even though your grandson is old enough to drive, you still think of him as a little kid. You think:

"He shouldn't be fastening his own seat belt. I should be buckling him in."

You're sure to embarrass him when he takes you for a drive.

"He had trouble learning his colors. How will he know when the light is red?"

"He always had his own way. He'll never obey a YIELD sign."

"He knows right from wrong. But does he know right from left?"

You'll never persuade your grandson to wait until next year to drive, but there are some things a concerned grandmother can do:

Have your car painted pink. He may be too embarrassed to drive in it.

Wear your dowdiest clothes so he won't want to be seen with you. When he asks you to duck down in the seat, do it. He'll be saved from embarrassment, and you'll be saved from seeing what's happening.

When he asks you to stop stepping on your imaginary brakes, tell him you are just keeping time to the music.

Tell him not to check his acne in the mirror while he's driving.

If he says, "Relax! I'll get you there on time," tell him you've got all day. Remind him that saving time isn't the issue—saving your life is.

Sometimes it's hard for a teen-ager to take learning to drive seriously. One grandmother told her grandson to put his hands on the steering wheel at the "quarter-to-three" position and he asked, "Does that change during daylight saving time?"

However, it isn't only grandchildren who make cute remarks during driving instructions. One grandmother asked her grandson, "Could we just stop at the doctor's a minute and see if he can get my heart started again?"

VIII
Your Presents
Will Be
Appreciated

Chapter 28

Yours Is Not to Reason Why, Yours Is But to Buy and Buy

"What did you bring me, Grandma?"
They ask when they are small.
They hope that you will answer,
"It's out in that big U-haul."

As a grandmother, I've learned that you can't buy love. But your grandchildren are disappointed when you don't try.

Would you throw a tantrum because your birthday present was a picture colored in kindergarten class? Of course not! But you can expect your grandchild to weep and wail if his gift from you is something you made in craft class at the Senior Citizen's Center.

Experienced grandmothers know you can't put too much time and effort into finding the right gifts for your grandchildren:

Go to rummage sales and notice which toys are the most beat-up. Those are the toys that children love to play with.

Watch a child with her mother in a store. Look at

what she's holding when her mother says, "Put that down!"

If you buy your grandson a drum, make sure it's too big for him to bring to your house when he comes.

Never buy from his first Christmas list. It is sure to be revised.

But don't worry if you buy him something he doesn't like. It hurts to be hugged too hard.

Once you've mastered the art of buying gifts the children like, there's another challenge—and it's a lot more difficult: getting your grandchildren out of a store without buying them something. You can try to drag them out, yelling and screaming, but with a little creativity, you can find easier ways:

Shop only at stores where you are familiar with the layout, so you don't risk walking into the toy department on the way to get what you need.

Make your granddaughter lie face down in the shopping cart, and tell her to look for pennies on the floor so she won't see anything she wants.

If she spots something she wants, say, "That will be out of style by the time we get home."

To get out of trouble in a hurry, say, "Let's walk to the front of the store and step on the magic spot that opens the door."

Or say that you have to get home fast because there are storm warnings out.

Once you've learned how to take your grandchildren to the store without buying them anything, you're home free. Remember: You can spend your entire Social Security check on a present, and his mother will still have to remind him, "What do you say to Grandma?"

Chapter 29

Over the River and Through the Woods Is Not Far Enough Away

At the turkey dinner,
It seems the greatest thrill
Is beating all the others
In making the biggest spill.

You probably don't remember ever jumping up, raising your hand, and saying, "It's my turn to have Thanksgiving at my house!" But come Thanksgiving, the entire family will be gathered around *your* dinner table.

It must be in the job description of grandmother. In fact, most grandmothers feel such a responsibility for their family's happiness on Thanksgiving Day that if they could, they would rig the traditional football game so the family's favorite team would win.

But don't expect the day to be storybook perfect. For instance, your giblets will get at least one: "Yuck, how gross!" You can also expect one: "Where are the French fries?," and your vegetarian daughter-in-law will look scornful through the

No matter what you serve on Thanksgiving, you'll hear complaints.

whole meal. One grandmother heard her grandson say, "This turkey's too stringy to eat, but save me a piece for after dinner—I'll floss my teeth with it."

There are two types of grandmothers—the ones who feel relieved when they hear the first "Let's go home" and the ones who feel hurt. The latter are definitely in the minority.

Here are some suggestions to help you have a happier Thanksgiving Day:

Make sure all the paper turkeys the grandchildren drew for you are fastened to the refrigerator door with magnets.

Either don't wear lipstick or make sure you kiss every grandchild if you kiss one.

When the number of grandchildren gets to 10, start using name tags. (You might as well add each child's grade in school.)

Remember which convenience stores are open, and send an unruly grandchild out to get something.

Don't look at the coats on the bed. You are bound to find at least one ripped lining that you feel you must sew.

If the piano bench has to be used for seating, nail it shut so it won't pinch fingers.

Consider buying a paper tablecloth. It sure beats washing and ironing a linen one.

Realize that if you use your good china, it may lose it's "good" status.

Start calling the family to eat at least a half hour before you want them at the table, because it will take that long to get them there.

Keep forcing food on them. If they eat enough, they'll become logy and inactive and won't wreck the house.

Have plenty of plastic bags to send leftovers home so no one will stay to eat supper.

Make sure you have jumper cables on hand for cars that might not start when you send them over the river and through the woods *back home.*

Chapter 30

Not a Tiny Tim Among Them

They invited you for Christmas,
And you'll head there through the drifts.
But wouldn't you have fainted
To read "Please omit the gifts"?

The realistic grandmother knows that Christmas can get completely out of control. Kids become wild. They throw tantrums when batteries don't come with toys. They ride their new bicycles in the house. You take your life in your hands when you walk through the house with its uncontrolled intersections.

But before you book a plane for Florida, consider that Grandmother plays a most important role in the family Christmas celebration. She's the one who sees to it that Christmas traditions are carried on. One grandmother told me her grandchildren didn't know they had to pop the popcorn before stringing it.

In order to enjoy Christmas with your grandchildren, you have to know what to expect:

There is nothing worse than thinking you are through shopping for a grandchild and then hearing that the toy you bought him has been recalled.

Kids would rather decorate each other with tinsel than the tree.

Telling them the real meaning of Christmas does not prevent them from crying when they don't get what they want.

When the toy that makes noise stops making noise, your grandchild will make noise.

If a child can tell that a gift contains clothing, he will not open it.

Kids will never win Oscars for pretending to be thankful for presents they don't like.

You can learn a lot from what experienced grandmothers say about Christmas with their grandchildren:

"I knew that I had waited too long to Christmas shop when I saw kids two blocks from the mall holding out signs that said 'PARK HERE.' "

"When you are buying presents for your grandchil-

Kids would rather decorate each other with tinsel than the tree.

dren on a fixed income, I think it's rotten when the parents want Santa to get credit for bringing them."

"On the flight out, I showed pictures of my grandchildren to all the passengers. On the flight home, I didn't even want to look at them myself."

"I put my back out holding him up so he could put the star on the top."

"The understatement of the year was when my daughter-in-law said: 'He's not one to gush.' "

"How she could tell the sweater was the wrong color by shaking the box, I'll never know."

"I know it's the thought that counts, but why did she make me a ceramic ashtray in art class when she knows I'm allergic to smoke?"

"I spent days making fruitcakes for them and all they said was, 'Yuck!' "

"We all held hands to sing 'Silent Night' and one grandchild dug his nail into his sister's hand so deeply she had to be taken to the emergency room."

"I explained to my grandson that the reason Baby Jesus didn't write 'Thank You' notes to the Wise Men was that He was a baby."

"I think it's better to be misty-eyed at the end of the phone than frazzled on the scene."

One grandmother drew up this list of suggestions for putting the Merry back into Christmas:

Suggest celebrating Christmas two weeks before or after, so the kids will be at school and have homework at night.

If you want Christmas stars to have all their points, deer to have antlers, Santas to have sacks, and Christmas trees to have tops, bake your Christmas cookies when your grandchildren are absent.

Be sure to know the latest spelling of your granddaughter's name before you sew the sequins on her Christmas stocking.

Ignore the mother when she tells you what the child needs.

Give presents that encourage the children to be outdoors while you are visiting, such as sleds, skis, ice skates, warm jackets, and a corncob pipe for a snowman.

Buy your grandchildren sweaters so they'll at least be quiet while pulling the sweaters over their heads.

To keep them busy and out of trouble, ask them to count fallen Christmas tree needles.

On Christmas morning, put carols on the stereo and turn the volume up full-blast to drown out the kids' complaints.

Videotape Christmas. If they see you aiming a camera at them, they may behave better.

Don't include self-addressed, stamped "Thank You" cards with the children's presents.

If you can't get together for a family Christmas celebration, here's something you'll wish they had at the post office: a line just for grandmothers sending Christmas packages, with chairs that move on a track toward the postal window.

Chapter 31

Don't Forget to Order a Corsage for Grandma

It used to be fun
To watch them romp.
Today you take pride
In their day of pomp.

Rites of passage aren't right if Grandma isn't there. One of the greatest contributions a grandmother makes is adding significance to an important event by her presence (and presents).

First Communion Is No Piece of Cake

Happy as she is at a grandchild's First Communion, a grandmother knows that formal occasions involving a child are fraught with danger. Typical First Communion worries include:

There may be horseplay in the vestibule, and your grandson will be pushed through the stained-glass door.

His shirttail will be out as he walks up to the altar.

Your granddaughter's slip will show as she walks up to the altar.

He'll step on the heel of the kid ahead of him.

She'll lose her front tooth on the communion wafer.

He'll blow a bubble just before the priest gives him communion.

He'll spill the wine he's carrying to the altar on the priest's white robe.

She'll stick her tongue out at her brother on the way back from communion.

Don't buy him any bubble gum for a week before his First Communion.

She'll scuff the toes of her patent leather shoes while she's kneeling.

When there is applause for the First Communicants after Mass, her brother will boo.

It's not easy to select an appropriate gift. You may feel a strong obligation to give a traditional religious gift—yet you also want to please the child. One solution is to give him a watch and say, "I'm giving you a watch so you can tell when it's time to go to church." Or give him a bicycle and say, "You're getting a bicycle so you won't be late for Mass."

A word of caution: On First Communion day, there will be many pictures taken and you will receive at least one. Don't place it near the phone! If you do, the next time your son calls to ask you to keep your grandchild for a week, you may glance at the picture of that angelic-looking child and end up saying "Yes."

Enjoy the Bar Mitzvah Buffet but Don't Burst a Button

Being present at the Bar Mitzvah of a grandson is one of the greatest thrills a grandmother can have. Just the other day, the Rabbi was at the lectern, frowning at your grandson, and now your grandson is at the lectern himself.

You've enjoyed listening to your grandson practice reading the Torah, getting ready for his big day. In fact, you were so proud, you called friends long distance to have them listen to him read. You even had him recite for the mailman.

Today he is a man. And you have to try extra hard to control yourself or you'll embarrass him:

Don't correct him from your seat if he mispronounces a word or sings off-key.

Don't give him a standing ovation when he finishes.

Don't tell him he has a crumb of honey cake on his lip—give him a kiss and get it off that way.

Your expectations for the Bar Mitzvah can be too high. Don't feel bad if he mentions his dog before you in the list of important influences in his life. And, although you probably thought he would make a face and spit out the wine, don't be upset when he licks his lips and smiles instead.

Finally, even though he is supposed to take responsibility from that moment forward, you can bet he won't change out of his new Bar Mitzvah suit before he joins in a touch football game when he gets home after the service.

If you don't expect too much at his Bar Mitzvah, you won't be disappointed.

Proms Are All-night Affairs

The senior prom is the biggest event of the year to many high school girls. Since it is so important, most girls want their grandmothers to share the excitement.

It is wonderful to see your granddaughter looking so beautiful in her formal. As you view her, you will understand why she hasn't eaten any cookies out of your cookie jar for the past three months.

Try not to embarrass her on prom night.

But proms also give grandmothers something to worry about. Staying out after prom until the wee hours used to mean staying out until 1 a.m. Now, the party doesn't break up until 9 a.m.

Grandmothers are often asked to go along on the prom shopping trip because mothers know two pocketbooks are better than one. Naturally, Grandma thinks the formal her granddaughter picks out is too revealing. But it doesn't help to remark, "Remember how drafty school gyms are, dear."

If your worries produce these desperate thoughts, forget them:

Prohibition can't be brought back for just one night.

Chaperones can't be bribed to keep an eye on your granddaughter.

Corsages aren't worn in the middle, no matter how

much cleavage there is. And the corsage can't be booby-trapped to prick her date if he gets too close.

Giving her a Bible and saying "This is for pressing your corsage" won't keep her from wrongdoing.

These comforting thoughts may lessen your concern:

She's so bare that she'll start sneezing, and he'll keep his distance.

The corridor gates in the school will be down, which will keep them out of the classrooms.

The band will drown out the "sweet nothings" he whispers into her ear.

If you feel courageous, here's some advice you may want to give your granddaughter:

Suggest to her that they dance every dance so he's too tired to try anything.

Inform her that she should not to be afraid of ruining her $25 manicure if he ceases to be a gentleman.

Remind her there will be photographers covering the event, so whatever they do might end up in the yearbook.

Tell her that the seat belt law applies even in parked cars.

To make your granddaughter's prom better for you, heed this advice:

Don't go near the house until she has adjusted to how her hair turned out at the beauty parlor.

Don't ask her escort about his father's occupation or his career plans.

Don't date yourself by saying, "Have a good time, Fred and Ginger!"

Don't show up at the restaurant where your granddaughter and her boyfriend are going to eat.

Don't take a dip in the school pool to cool off.

Graduation—You're Not
Getting Older, They Are!

It is always so hot on Graduation Day that many grand-mothers harbor the secret hope that their grandchild does not go on to college so they won't have to sit through another graduation.

Graduations are similar to the Academy Awards: One student usually sweeps the awards. This is very boring, unless your grandchild is the big winner.

If you don't know what to worry about, try these typical graduation anxieties:

Her gown will fly open and show shockingly short shorts.

His tassle will hypnotize him and he'll be asleep when his name is called.

A flashbulb will blind her and she'll fall down the steps after getting her diploma.

She won't remember to say "Thank you" when she is handed her diploma.

A grandmother who wants to come off well at a graduation should heed the following suggestions:

Don't take a dip in the school pool to cool off.

Don't leave right after your grandchild receives his or her diploma.

Don't say, "I paid your library fine so you could graduate. That is my graduation present."

Don't pretend you have fainted just to get the graduation speaker to stop talking.

Don't wave back to your grandchild until you make sure she is waving to you. She is probably waving to her boyfriend's family sitting nearby.

Wedding Bell Blues

It is always hard to believe that your grandchild is old enough to get married. When you look at the wedding matchbooks with the children's names, you'll think it was just a short time ago that you scolded him for playing with matches. And as you gaze at your granddaughter in her wedding gown, you'll recall it was just the other day that you bought her bridal cutouts to play with.

Grandmothers are sure to worry. If your grandson is getting married, you'll think, "I wish they'd stop telling her how beautiful she is—she'll think she's too good for him." If it's

Grandmothers can always find something to worry about at the wedding.

your granddaughter, you'll fret, "Who could have written 'Sucker' on the soles of the shoes of the man getting my precious granddaughter?"

A little forethought can increase your enjoyment of the wedding and reduce potential friction:

Try to talk your granddaughter out of an outdoor wedding. Artificial light is much more flattering to a grandmother than sunlight.

Don't sign the guest book "NaNa," even if that's what the bride calls you.

Don't offer to tend bar at the reception.

No matter how tired you get, don't ask if you can use the ring bearer's pillow to take a nap.

Don't be shocked by the band. You shouldn't expect Bob Crosby and the Bob Cats.

Throw the rice underhand. An overhand throw shows more arm flab.

Finally, consider your grandchild has married well if one of her new in-laws asks if you are the bride's aunt.

A Final Thought

Despite all the worries and problems, being a grandmother does provide a lot of pleasure. When your grandchild reaches up to take your hand, you are in heaven, even if you are being led down the aisle of the toy department.

The Very Best Baby Name Book in the Whole Wide World

by Bruce Lansky

Compiled by Bruce Lansky, the world's #1 author of baby name books, this book provides more helpful information than any other book.

Order #1030

The Best Baby Shower Book

by Courtney Cooke

Who says baby showers have to be dull? This contemporary guide for planning baby showers is packed with helpful hints, recipes, decorating ideas, and activities that are fun without being juvenile.

Order #1239

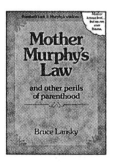

Mother Murphy's Law

by Bruce Lansky

The wit of Bombeck and the wisdom of Murphy are combined in this illustrated collection of 325 "laws" that detail the perils and pitfalls of parenthood. Sales of translation rights in 10 foreign countries prove the universality of Lansky's humor.

Order #1149

Moms Say the Funniest Things!

by Bruce Lansky

Bruce Lansky has collected all the greatest lines moms have ever used to deal with such "emergencies" as getting the kids out of bed in the morning, cleaned, dressed, to school, to the dinner table, undressed, and back to bed. A fun gift for mom and the rest of the family, too.

Order #4280

Dads Say the Dumbest Things!

by Bruce Lansky & K.L. Jones

Here's a hilarious book that has every funny (and stupid) expression fathers use to educate and discipline their children...and drive them up the wall. It also includes 19 photos of TV's favorite fathers, plus humorous quotes from their TV shows.

Order #4220

Familiarity Breeds Children

selected by Bruce Lansky

This collection of the cleverest and most outrageous quotes and cartoons about raising children has been repackaged to make it an even more appealing gift for parents new and old. Includes the best of yesterday's and today's humorists.

Order #4015

What's So Funny about Getting Old

by Jane Thomas Noland
illustrated by Ed Fischer

Do you know somebody who needs some good-natured ribbing about their "advancing age"? Here's a gag gift that will liven up the birthday party of anyone too old to be a member of generation X. If you know someone whose "head makes promises their body can't possibly keep," you must buy them this book.

Order #4205

Grandma's Favorite Photos

Help Grandma proudly show off her grandkids with this handsome photo album. It will become the most paged-through book in her home.

Order #3109

Age Happens

selected by Bruce Lansky

A compilation of the funniest things ever said or written about growing older by the most insightful wits of all time, including Ellen DeGeneris, Garrison Keillor, Bill Cosby, and many more! This book includes 15 cartoons by some of *The New Yorker's* most popular cartoonists.

Order #4025

Joy of Grandparenting

by Audrey Sherins and Joan Holleman
This book will have grandparents smiling in agreement as they read these modern proverbs.

Order #3502

Happy Helpful Grandma Guide

by Leslie Spirson and Clair Lehr, Ph.D.
This book celebrates grandparenting from two perspectives—those of the grandparent and parent. It offers insightful advice on such issues as building a happy and healthy relationship between three generations; relating to in-laws without becoming an outlaw; creating new family traditions; and redefining oneself at a new stage of life.

Order #1290

Are You Over the Hill?

by Bill Dodds
illustrated by Stephen Carpenter
Jam-packed with fun ways to remind old codgers or 34 or more that their better years are behind them. A great gag gift for friends' and family members' birthdays.

Order #4265

Order Form

Qty	Title	Author	Order No.	Unit Cost (U.S. $)	Total
	Age Happens	Lansky, B.	4025	$7.00	
	Are You Over the Hill?	Dodds, B.	4265	$6.00	
	Best Baby Name Book	Lansky, B.	1029	$5.00	
	Best Baby Shower Book	Cooke, C.	1239	$7.00	
	Dads Say the Dumbest Things!	Lansky/Jones	4220	$6.00	
	Familiarity Breeds Children	Lansky, B.	4015	$7.00	
	For Better And For Worse	Lansky, B.	4000	$7.00	
	Grandma Knows Best	McBride, M.	4009	$7.00	
	Grandma's Favorite Photos		3109	$8.00	
	Happy Helpful Grandma Guide	Spirson, L.	1290	$8.00	
	Italian without Words	Carpini, C. & D.	5100	$6.00	
	Joy of Grandparenting	Sherins/Holleman	3502	$7.00	
	Moms Say the Funniest Things!	Lansky, B.	4280	$6.00	
	Mother Murphy's Law	Lansky, B.	1149	$5.00	
	Over-the-Hill Party Game Book	Cooke, C.	6062	$3.95	
	Practical Parenting Tips	Lansky, V.	1180	$8.00	
	Very Best Baby Name Book	Lansky, B.	1030	$8.00	
	What's So Funny about Getting Old?	Noland, J.	4205	$7.00	
				Subtotal	
			Shipping and Handling (see below)		
			MN residents add 6.5% sales tax		
				Total	

YES, please send me the books indicated above. Add $2.00 shipping and handling for the first book and 50¢ for each additional book. Add $2.50 to total for books shipped to Canada. Overseas postage will be billed. Allow up to four weeks for delivery. Send check or money order payable to Meadowbrook Press. No cash or C.O.D.'s, please. Prices subject to change without notice. **Quantity discounts available upon request.**

Send book(s) to:

Name _____ Phone _____

Address _____

City _____ State _____ Zip _____

Payment via:

❏ Check or money order payable to Meadowbrook Press. (No cash or C.O.D.'s please.)

Amount enclosed $ _____

❏ Visa (for orders over $10.00 only)   ❏ MasterCard (for orders over $10.00 only)

Account # _____

Signature _____ Exp. Date _____

A **FREE** Meadowbrook Press catalog is available upon request.
You can also phone us for orders of $10.00 or more at 1-800-338-2232

Mail to: Meadowbrook Press
5451 Smetana Drive, Minnetonka, MN 55343

Phone (612) 930-1100   Toll-Free 1-800-338-2232   Fax (612) 930-1940